Little People, BIG DREAMS

MARTIN LUTHER KING JR.

Written by
Maria Isabel Sánchez Vegara

Illustrated by
Mai Ly Degnan

Frances Lincoln
Children's Books

Little Martin was a spiritual boy from Atlanta who came from a long line of preachers. His dad was a preacher, his uncle was a preacher, his grandfather was a preacher... maybe he'd become a great preacher, too.

One day, a friend invited him over to play. Martin was shocked when he was asked to leave because he was black. That day, he realised something terrible was going on.

This terrible thing was called 'segregation'. It meant that public places — like restaurants and buses — had separate spaces for black and white people. Martin and his friend were sent to different schools.

Martin believed that one shouldn't remain silent or accept something if it's wrong. He promised himself that when he grew up, he'd fight injustice with the most powerful weapon of all: words.

Martin studied at universities in Georgia, Pennsylvania and Massachusetts, where he read about Mahatma Gandhi – the man who had improved the lives of millions of Indians with peaceful methods of protest.

When he finished his studies, Martin moved to Alabama and became the pastor of a church in Montgomery. Every Sunday, from his pulpit, he encouraged his congregation to speak up about things that mattered.

One evening, a woman called Rosa was arrested for
refusing to give up her seat to a white man on a bus.
Martin asked the people in his community not
to take the bus again until the law was changed.

Many citizens were inspired by Rosa's story and Martin's words. Suddenly, buses were almost empty! They stayed empty for more than a year, until segregation on Montgomery's buses finally ended.

It was the first major civil rights action in America... but not the last. Martin encouraged people all over the country to stand up for their rights and join in with peaceful protest.

They were often attacked and Martin was arrested twenty-nine times. But he and his followers never fought back with force.

He knew that hate can't drive out hate;
only love can.

Martin helped to organise a protest march on Washington where he gave a life-changing speech. It began with four simple yet powerful words: "I have a dream".

The next year, Martin became the youngest person to win The Nobel Peace Prize. His words of hope, peace and justice called a nation to change its laws and make them equal for everyone.

And if you listen to your heart, you can still hear little Martin asking you to keep his dream alive.

A dream of a world where we are judged by
our character, not by the colour of our skin.

I HAVE A DREAM

MARTIN LUTHER KING JR.

(Born 1929 • Died 1968)

1953

1956

Martin Luther King Junior was born 'Michael', in Atlanta, Georgia, but later changed his name to Martin. Growing up in a family of pastors, Martin quickly learned to tell the difference between right and wrong. His happy childhood gave him what he later called a "strong determination for justice", and an optimism that cut through the segregated world he was born into. When he was old enough to leave home to go to university, he combined studies of religion with the teachings of Gandhi – a leading activist who chose to protest with peaceful demonstration, not violence. Martin learned from this, and discovered that his writing – and speeches – were the best ways to change people's hearts and minds. One of his first opportunities to do

1963   1965

so was as pastor of the Dexter Avenue Baptist Church in Montgomery, Alabama. There, his passionate sermons inspired a new sense of hope. At the same time, he also became the leader of the first African American non-violent demonstration, started by Rosa Parks, known as the 'bus boycott'. The protest lasted 382 days, and following that time, the Supreme Court of the United States declared that both black and white Americans should ride the buses as equals. Over the next ten years, Martin travelled more than six million miles, catching the attention of the world with his dream where children would "not be judged by the colour of their skin but by the content of their character." Martin's dream continues to inspire us to action today.

Want to find out more about **Martin Luther King Jr.?**
Have a read of these great books:

I Have a Dream by Kadir Nelson
Martin's Big Words: The Life of Martin Luther King, Jr. by Doreen Rappaport

Brimming with creative inspiration, how-to projects, and useful information to enrich your everyday life, Quarto Knows is a favourite destination for those pursuing their interests and passions. Visit our site and dig deeper with our books into your area of interest: Quarto Creates, Quarto Cooks, Quarto Homes, Quarto Lives, Quarto Drives, Quarto Explores, Quarto Gifts, or Quarto Kids.

Text © 2020 Maria Isabel Sánchez Vegara. Illustrations © 2020 Mai Ly Degnan.
First Published in the UK in 2020 by Frances Lincoln Children's Books, an imprint of The Quarto Group.
The Old Brewery, 6 Blundell Street, London N7 9BH, United Kingdom.
T (0)20 7700 6700 F (0)20 7700 8066 **www.QuartoKnows.com**
First Published in Spain in 2019 under the title Pequeño & Grande Martin Luther King, Jr.
by Alba Editorial, s.l.u., Baixada de Sant Miquel, 1, 08002 Barcelona
www.albaeditorial.es
All rights reserved.
Published by arrangement with Alba Editorial, s.l.u. Translation rights arranged by IMC Agència Literària, SL
All rights reserved.

A catalogue record for this book is available from the British Library.
ISBN 978-0-7112-4566-2
Set in Futura BT.

Published by Katie Cotton • Designed by Karissa Santos
Edited by Rachel Williams and Katy Flint • Production by Nicolas Zeifman

Manufactured in Guangdong, China CC082020

9 7 5 3 4 6 8

Photographic acknowledgements (pages 28-29, from left to right) 1. Martin Luther King, 1953 © Michael Evans / Hulton Archive via Getty Images 2. Martin Luther King mug shot, 1956 © Kypros via Getty 3. Martin Luther King, Jr. March on Washington, 1963 © Hulton Deutsch via Getty 4. March from Selma to Alabama, 1965 © Stephen F. Somerstein via Getty

Collect the
Little People, **BIG DREAMS** series:

FRIDA KAHLO

ISBN: 978-1-84780-770-0

COCO CHANEL

ISBN: 978-1-84780-771-7

MAYA ANGELOU

ISBN: 978-1-84780-890-5

AMELIA EARHART

ISBN: 978-1-84780-885-1

AGATHA CHRISTIE

ISBN: 978-1-84780-959-9

MARIE CURIE
ISBN: 978-1-84780-961-2

ROSA PARKS

ISBN: 978-1-78603-017-7

AUDREY HEPBURN

ISBN: 978-1-78603-052-8

EMMELINE PANKHURST

ISBN: 978-1-78603-019-1

ELLA FITZGERALD

ISBN: 978-1-78603-086-3

ADA LOVELACE

ISBN: 978-1-78603-075-7

JANE AUSTEN

ISBN: 978-1-78603-119-8

GEORGIA O'KEEFFE

ISBN: 978-1-78603-121-1

HARRIET TUBMAN

ISBN: 978-1-78603-289-8

ANNE FRANK

ISBN: 978-1-78603-292-8

MOTHER TERESA

ISBN: 978-1-78603-290-4

JOSEPHINE BAKER

ISBN: 978-1-78603-291-1

L. M. MONTGOMERY

ISBN: 978-1-78603-295-9

JANE GOODALL

ISBN: 978-1-78603-294-2

SIMONE DE BEAUVOIR

ISBN: 978-1-78603-293-5

MUHAMMAD ALI

ISBN: 978-1-78603-733-6

STEPHEN HAWKING

ISBN: 978-1-78603-732-9

MARIA MONTESSORI

ISBN: 978-1-78603-753-4

VIVIENNE WESTWOOD

ISBN: 978-1-78603-756-5

MAHATMA GANDHI

ISBN: 978-1-78603-334-5

DAVID BOWIE

ISBN: 978-1-78603-803-6

WILMA RUDOLPH

ISBN: 978-1-78603-750-3

DOLLY PARTON

ISBN: 978-1-78603-759-6

BRUCE LEE

ISBN: 978-1-78603-335-2

RUDOLF NUREYEV

ISBN: 978-1-78603-336-9

ZAHA HADID

ISBN: 978-1-78603-744-2

MARY SHELLEY

ISBN: 978-1-78603-747-3

MARTIN LUTHER KING JR.

ISBN: 978-0-7112-4566-2

DAVID ATTENBOROUGH

ISBN: 978-0-7112-4563-1

ASTRID LINDGREN

ISBN: 978-1-78603-762-6

EVONNE GOOLAGONG

ISBN: 978-0-7112-4585-3

BOB DYLAN

ISBN: 978-0-7112-4674-4

ALAN TURING

ISBN: 978-0-7112-4677-5

BILLIE JEAN KING

ISBN: 978-0-7112-4692-8

GRETA THUNBERG

ISBN: 978-0-7112-5643-9

JESSE OWENS

ISBN: 978-0-7112-4582-2

JEAN-MICHEL BASQUIAT
ISBN: 978-0-7112-4579-2

ARETHA FRANKLIN

ISBN: 978-0-7112-4687-4

CORAZON AQUINO

ISBN: 978-0-7112-4683-6

PELÉ

ISBN: 978-0-7112-4574-7

ERNEST SHACKLETON

ISBN: 978-0-7112-4570-9

STEVE JOBS

ISBN: 978-0-7112-4576-1

AYRTON SENNA

ISBN: 978-0-7112-4671-3

LOUISE BOURGEOIS

ISBN: 978-0-7112-4689-8

ELTON JOHN

ISBN: 978-0-7112-5838-9